AF674291

Fal

Gereneicia Darrenét

BookLeaf Publishing

Fall © 2022 Gereneicia Darrenét

All rights reserved.

No part of this publication may be reproduced, stored in a retrieval system, or transmitted, in any form or by any means, electronic, mechanical, photocopying, recording or otherwise, without the prior written permission of the presenters.

Gereneicia Darrenét asserts the moral right to be identified as author of this work.

Presentation by *BookLeaf Publishing*

Web: www.bookleafpub.com

E-mail: info@bookleafpub.com

ISBN: 9789357617307

First edition 2022

I dedicate this book to my children but I want to send a special shout out to my daughter Trinity. I will never forget that cold, winter trip to the doctor when you whispered from the back seat, "Mom, you need to write a book." Well here is my first one! Thank you for encouraging me and always believing in me. I love each of you!

ACKNOWLEDGEMENT

I want to acknowledge Jesus. Thank you for loving me and giving me this gift of writing. All of this is for You, to You and from You.

PREFACE

This mini collection was birthed on a whim as I was perusing social media. There it was! This invitation to write 21 days of Poetry and have it published. I said to myself, "I need to do something that will challenge me and awaken my hunger to write again." Then I looked up and said, " I want this to be between You and I and no one else. I want this journey to honor You." Then I dove in daily just to be vulnerable with the lover of my soul in a series of short expressive explosions of words.

Some days it reads from me to Him, others from Him to me and/or just an excerpt from a day in the life. No matter what it was always about my relationship with Him. I hope you see that expressed here, the pain, joy, comfort, real and rawness of each piece as I walked through a difficult season of transition.

PREFACE

TEARS

The language of the soul

Tiny

Expressive

Powerful

Released to break the glaciers in my mind

To flood the deserts that have populated my soul

To stir this broken heart

Yet, they seem to fail

But…

Oh, what you can do with these distraught drops

Beauty for ashes

Joy in the morning

Refreshment

Restoration

The streams that flow from these eyelids

Jesus

In Your hands

Are like a wild waterfall that cascades and feeds
a jungle

I entrust these tears to

You

WAVES

How is this pain and peace simultaneous?

The pain crashes in waves

But the peace is steady

An underlying current

Unseen yet undeniable

Constant and consistent

The pain is suffocating

Infuriating

It's like water

Powerful. Needed

And the oil of peace is the current

Timely nourishment

The waves can't sway or rupture the current

The water cannot penetrate the oil

The waves crash but I allow the current to

Pull me away.

The waves submerge me

But I'm not drowning

With the current there is abundance

And You are my anchor

LET GO

I Keep waiting for something to change.

Supernatural

Shift

Miracle

And there's nothing but this hole in my chest

Emptiness

I feel the tug to let go

And

I believe I have released

But then

Constriction

Fear

Unknown

Re-grip

How do I let go?

When will I be okay?

These feelings yet valid are not THE truth

Your truth says be still and know

So teach me to let go

REALITY

It’s

Somewhere between truth and perception

Our focus

Our space

Where we live, breathe and exist

But it can become

Tarnished

Weighed down

Reality meets life expectations

Greeting others’ views

Accepts cultural pitfalls

Embraces worldly obsessions

& Melds into disarray

But

You are not the author of confusion

You hold me and Your truth secure

In your palm

Your reality transforms mine

And I know I don't have to wonder

Shift or convert

My existence is what you made

I'm made real by You

RAGE

The seasons must change

But

That doesn't mean they come calmly

The anger seethes

A fiery flame

A bittersweet salve to the sadness

Don't know what to do with the lava flow of fury

Except

Surrender

Allow it to propel me forward

So thankful that You take what the enemy meant for evil

And

Use it ALL for good

This temper is temporary

Your love is eternal

And

Extinguishes every wrong flame

Let the fire in these eyes reflect Your joy

The inferno in this heart swell with your peace

You hold me tight in the furnace

I trust You

IMPARTATION

The sweet incomparable gift of transfer

Of your Spirit

Peace, love, joy…AND

STRENGTH

It fills my lungs with every breath, orders every step

EMPOWERED

By a Holy Love

That I don't deserve

But Grace

And obedience from Your flock that I receive

So much more than I could fathom

Renewed

From broken to surety

Hopeless to hope

Confusion to knowing…

Your word says where two or three are gathered

You are in the midst
Thank you

My Beginning…my End…

But mostly my everything right here in

My middle

GRIEF

The pendulum swing

From the power highs to the ultimate lows

Conundrum

Why does this hurt so bad

The comfortable is cozy

But this place is cold

Uncomfortable seems too hard

Yet, necessary

The tears sting the corners of my eyes

I trust You

Questions swell on my tongue

Again, I trust you

My heart aches in my chest

Still, I trust You

Can this cup pass from me?

But not my will but Yours

Let it be well with my soul…

Some way…Some how

I trust You

GRACE

Tethered to this goodness

It doesn't make sense…

Where would I be had You not carried me

Parted the waters

Spoke to the storms

This is more than courteous goodwill

This is divine kindness

Bestowed by The King

Who chose me before I could speak

Numbered each hair on my head

Allows me to graze his thoughts more than there
is sand on the shore

Called me by name

There are no words for the graciousness You are

As my heart swells

All I can murmur is…

Thank you

REDIRECTION

Yesterday

I went on a walk with You

Listened to the wind whisper through the leaves

Heard water birds serenade the sunrise

Felt the faint kiss of fall on my skin

Immersed myself in the morning mundane

As I poured my tears and fears to you

Gently

Lovingly

You whispered

"The path you were on was leading to destruction…

I must take you on this journey because for so long you have been loved wrong &

You won't let my love in…"

I understand El Roi{The God who sees me}
That this disruption isn't punishment

But a loving redirection

I trust You

RAIN

I wish it would rain

Storm

The sky pours her tears in wild vengeance,
cascades over the landscapes

The thunder roars his declaration of war

The lightning singes the clouds in bright anger

Then my surroundings would match how I feel
inside

My soul screaming for relief

Tarnished by the constant pain

Burned by rejection

The denial changes you

Thought I was healed but I've just been broken
anew

Glad that I have Your truth as my reassurance,

THAT

“You are close the broken hearted and saves
those who are crushed in spirit…
You bind up their wounds

Rain down your fury of love Gracious Tempest

Put me back together

Rightly

Healed & whole

FAIR

My son mumbled those words to me from the back seat yesterday

As he combed through his feelings about the reality of our new circumstances

I tried to condense as much of this 35-year-old wisdom into 9-year-old verbiage he could comprehend

I am not sure if he understood or even if I do

Truth is I've muttered those same words to you, today to be exact

I grumbled about the existence of pain

I wept about the losses

Fought the frustration, shame and unfairness of it all

You couldn't possibly know how I feel

Oh, but you do
You gently reminded that You have experienced my deep grief

While you hung on a cross, the weight of my heaviness was on You

I sobbed an apology to You

You whispered to my heart, “I did it so you could be healed.”

Your presence cupped my tear-stained face and breathed into me,

“You were worth it.”

FALL

Beautiful dying

All around me

Creation succumbs to the shifting

In a brilliant display of reds, oranges, yellows
and browns

The air has a kiss of coolness

The trees release their seasonal friends

As they steady themselves for winter

There is glory in liberation

Magnificence in how there is death now

But new life awaits

El Shaddai carry me in this season

Open my eyes to the gracious dying that You are
allowing in and around me

I surrender to it, to You

Be my foundation to stand on in the wilds of winter

And I wait with expectation for spring to blossom in my soul

I will be like a well-watered garden…

Restored.

COURAGE

The strength to move on

To adapt

Venture into the deep

With seemingly no rescue in sight

The drive to push past the waves

Glide amongst the riptides

Face the storm

Resilience

It all comes from You

The well in the depths of my soul

That says "Don't give up! Don't give in!

The storm looks ominous

Endless

But there is a rainbow close”

I know

You won’t call me where You won’t go

I will never voyage alone

My heart echoes Your commands,

“…Be strong and courageous

Do not be afraid or discouraged

For my Lord, my God is with me wherever I go”

I trust you

CHAMPION

Peace. Creator. Living Water. The Beginning.
Hope. Love.

Amazing. Merciful. Gracious. Perfection.
Unfailing. Glorious. Redeemer.

Generous. Strong Tower. Anchor.

Great. Magnificent. Waymaker. Joy. Powerful.

Blessing. Omnipotent. Mysterious.
Overwhelming. Deep. Consuming Fire.

Illuminator. Life-giving. Strength. Holy.

Precious. Revealing. Timeless. Worthy. Provider.
Miracle Working.

Omniscient. Promise keeper. Present.

I AM

My everything, forever

That's who You are

THE DEEP

Daughter, you think I have called you out here to flail in the surf?

Be sucked into the tide?

Drowned by the waves and currents?

To leave you? No.

I lead you out here to learn, be reshaped and shift

Posture

Out here in these storms you learn the weight of My anchor

You feel the truth of my presence

And understand the necessity of the wait. In your weakness when you can no longer swim

You will discover My strength

You will learn to swim differently than you did in the shallows

You can tread with confidence here because I AM your sure thing that keeps you afloat

Flail? Fail? With me?!

Never.

Out here I AM your source, and you will

Flourish

WORSHIP

I don't have much to offer except these shattered pieces

My voice is barely a whisper

My body is fatigued

My mind is exhausted

My will seemingly gone

But

I will allow every breath to honor You

I was made to praise You

These tears are my song of

Heartbreak and breakthrough

Losses and victory

This brokenness is my offering

Because…oh…

What the Potter can do with these broken pieces

You use these shards to strengthen the new jar

You breathe new life into these dry bones

You desire a broken and contrite heart

Oh, you won't despise me

I bring all that I am here to your feet in humility

Surrender

At the end of me

I have found You

JOY

I know you don't believe it and can't even perceive

the blessing that will be birthed here

What's coming to fruition

The joy in the morning

I know all you see is pain and here at end of you…

you don't understand Me

But oh, count it all joy

If you could see what I see

If only you knew my sweet love

you'd sink deeper into My joy

So, I urge you

I challenge you to press past the uncomfortable

And fall into the pillows of My presence

Everything you need is right here

And everything out there, your future, is tucked safely in my palms

Indulge in

Meditate on

Drink from the well of joy

It is My promise and your strength

WARRIOR

I feel it

Surging through my veins, coursing inside of me

I sense the build of momentum

The battle at its peak

I cry out

Lift my voice and hands in wild abandon

The breakthrough is just beyond the bend

I can't see it, but my soul knows

The tears were not wasted

The pain was just a brilliant pathway

The scars speak a new language of love

The war paint glistens as sweat beads on my
brow and kisses each color

Tears of joy pool in my open palms

Redemption

I am ready to receive

I have dropped my weapons for this battle was never mine

But I accept the gift of victory

KNOW YOU

Forgive me

I have been distracted

Allowed myself to be pulled

many different way and places

Listened to a multitude of voices

And ultimately questioned Yours

I have tried in my own strength

Trusted the wrong abilities

But each path leads me back to You

I know there's nothing that can satisfy like You

There is no place I can go that you won't follow

When I draw near…there You are

You are matchless

And…I need to know You

I invite you into this place…

My heart…as it longs for Yours

Come and do only what You can do

Breathe on me

Wash me in the water of Your word

Clothe me in unfailing love

I need You

ABIDE

There are new levels that I am calling you to

Beyond your understanding, recognition, and comprehension

It will require radical obedience

Uncomfortableness

But know you can rest in my infinite grace

Remember you are tethered to my unfailing love

I am with You

Calling you to be with me

This is a divine pursuit for your heart

Will you release it to me? Permit me to hold you close?

Will you be open to forgiveness, discipline and real love…

Agape love?

This journey will be worth it

FREE

Jesus, I want to be free

And I am unsure of what that looks like

But I know that true freedom is found in You

Uninhibited

Breath taking

Release

My daughter…

Every step you take with me is a step towards liberty

Every surrender

Every whisper of forgiveness

Every posture of humility, thanksgiving, and praise

Is in invitation for the open doors of heaven to rain down abundance

Abundance in hope, peace, grace, mercy

Continue in your pursuit of me

You don't have to earn your keep here

You are always welcome

And my promises are always yes and amen

For whom I set free is free indeed

Be free

www.ingramcontent.com/pod-product-compliance
Lightning Source LLC
Chambersburg PA
CBHW062203160726
48282CB00027B/971
* 9 7 8 9 3 5 7 6 1 7 3 0 7 *